The MAILBOX®

Ready for January & February

Practical and Fun Activities for Timely Themes

- ☐ New Year's Day
- ☐ Snow
- ☐ Mittens
- ☐ Arctic Animals
- ☐ Martin Luther King Day

- ☐ Dental Health
- ☐ Valentine's Day
- ☐ Groundhog Day

Managing Editor: Kimberly Ann Brugger

Editorial Team: Becky S. Andrews, Diane Badden, Janet Boyce, Tricia Kylene Brown, Kimberley Bruck, Karen A. Brudnak, Catherine Caudill, Clare Cox, Pam Crane, Chris Curry, Roxanne LaBell Dearman, David Drews, Brenda Fay, Ada Goren, Tazmen Fisher Hansen, Marsha Heim, Lori Z. Henry, Cindy Hoying, Suzanne Moore, Tina Petersen, Mark Rainey, Greg D. Rieves, Mary Robles, Deborah J. Ryan, Rebecca Saunders, Donna K. Teal, Sharon M. Tresino, Norinne Weeks, Zane Williard

www.themailbox.com

©2014 The Mailbox® Books
All rights reserved.
ISBN 978-1-61276-436-8

Printed in The United States
10 9 8 7 6 5 4 3 2 1

HPS252117

Table of Contents

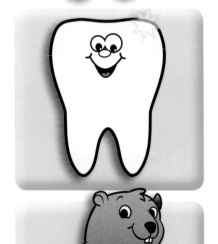

What's Inside

Group Time

Brand-new ideas!

Centers

Just what you need to be ready for

January and February!

Songs & Such

Arts & Crafts

Patterns

Tear-Out Teaching Tools

Group Time

A Noisy Time

Participating in a group activity

Use a large clock manipulative to show students the time of 12:00. Explain that at 12:00 AM on January 1, people around the world celebrate the beginning of a new year. Give each child a handheld noisemaker. Then display a variety of times on the clock. Each time you show 12:00, prompt each student to use his noisemaker.

Janet Boyce
Cokato, MN

Last year I...	This year I want to...
met Mickey Mouse saw a parade went to the beach	ride my bike go camping see my grandma

Looking Back and Forward

Oral language

Youngsters will enjoy sharing memories of the past year and memories to be made in the upcoming year. Prepare a chart like the one shown. To begin, write a favorite memory from the past year on the chart and share it with students. Then encourage youngsters to share memories of the past year. Write their words in the appropriate column. Next, write and share about something you want to do in the upcoming year. Then record students' thoughts about what they want to do in the upcoming year.

Mary Robles, Portland, OR

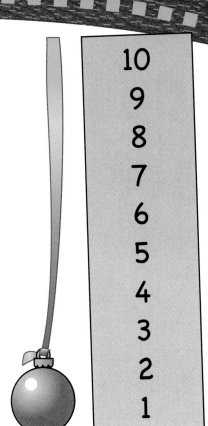

New Year's Countdown

Counting backward from ten

Post a long paper strip programmed like the one shown. Attach a length of ribbon to an unbreakable ornament and place it near the strip. Share the tradition of the ball drop in Times Square. Then invite your youngsters to join in a classroom ball drop. Hold the ball next to the number 10 and direct students to crouch down. Lower the ball as you lead the group in counting. After the group says "one," students jump up and shout, "Happy New Year!"

Janet Boyce
Cokato, MN

Warm Winter Wear

The season of winter

Reinforce how to dress for winter weather with this entertaining activity. Place several articles of winter clothing and a few summer items in a box (or suitcase). Invite a child to take an item from the box and show it to the group. Then lead youngsters in singing the song below, inserting the name of the item in the third line. At the end of the song, discuss whether the item is appropriate winter wear. Continue with the remaining items.

(sung to the tune of "Clementine")

When it's winter and it's snowing
And you want to go and play,
Would [these sandals] keep you cozy?
Would they keep the cold away?

Suzanne Moore
Tucson, AZ

Group Time

Handy Fashions
Data analysis

Do your little ones prefer gloves or mittens? Find out with this fun activity. Invite each child to put on her mittens or gloves. (Have a few extra pairs for students who need them.) In turn, invite each child to stand and model her hand wear. Then help youngsters sort themselves into two groups based on hand wear. Help students count each group and then compare the groups using words like *more*, *less*, and *equal*.

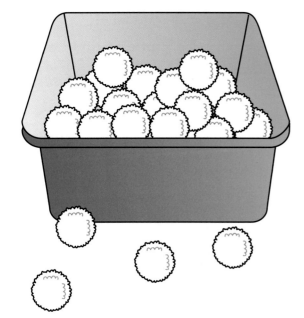

Gathering Snowflakes
Counting

Place a tub of white pom-poms (snowflakes) near your group-time area. Invite students to put on their gloves or mittens. (Have a few extra pairs of mittens or gloves handy for students who need them.) Recite the rhyme shown as you walk around the group dropping snowflakes. At the end of the rhyme, have each youngster gather a set of three snowflakes. Direct each child to count his snowflakes aloud as he returns them to the tub. Play several rounds of this game, substituting a different number each time.

Snowing here, snowing there,
Snowing all around.
Find [three] snowflakes
On the ground.

Cindy Hoying, Centerville, OH

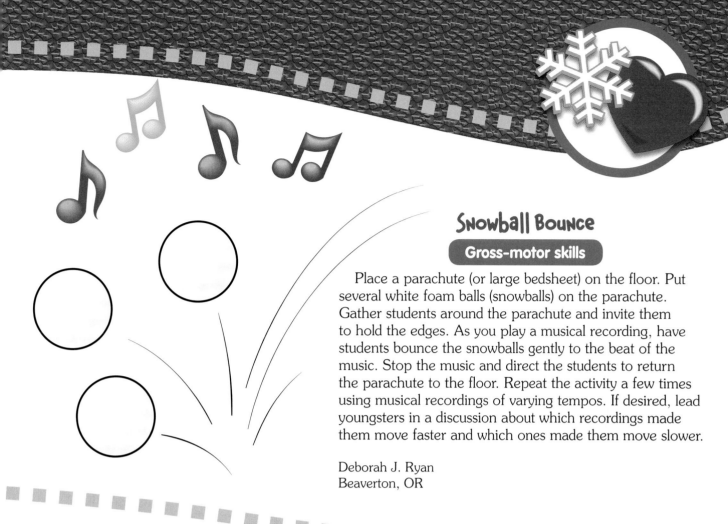

Snowball Bounce

Gross-motor skills

Place a parachute (or large bedsheet) on the floor. Put several white foam balls (snowballs) on the parachute. Gather students around the parachute and invite them to hold the edges. As you play a musical recording, have students bounce the snowballs gently to the beat of the music. Stop the music and direct the students to return the parachute to the floor. Repeat the activity a few times using musical recordings of varying tempos. If desired, lead youngsters in a discussion about which recordings made them move faster and which ones made them move slower.

Deborah J. Ryan
Beaverton, OR

Gliding Along

Letter recognition

Arrange a class supply of large letter cards on the floor (ice-skating rink), leaving plenty of room between them. Lead youngsters in pretending to put on their winter wear and ice skates. Then play a lively musical recording and have little ones "ice-skate" around the letter cards. Stop the music and have each student stand near a letter card. Name a letter and direct the child standing near the card to do a fancy twirl on her pretend ice skates. Continue for several rounds.

adapted from an idea by Deborah J. Ryan

Penelope Penguin's Trip

Letter sound /p/

Cut apart a copy of the cards on pages 16 and 17. Then arrange the penguin card and the word card in a pocket chart as shown. Place the picture cards facedown in lower pockets. Set a small bag near the pocket chart. Explain that Penelope Penguin is packing for a big trip but can only pack things that begin with /p/. Invite a volunteer to choose a card, flip it over, and place it after the word card. Lead the group in reading the rebus sentence. If the item's name begins with /p/, have a volunteer place the card in the bag. If it does not, have him set the card aside. Continue with the remaining cards. After all the cards have been used, review the items that Penelope packed for her trip.

Ada Goren
Winston-Salem, NC

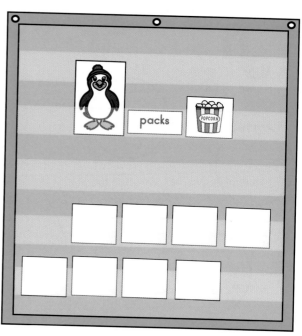

packs

Balance the Egg

Animal characteristics

Gather a supply of plastic eggs. To begin, tell students that king and emperor penguins don't place their eggs in nests like most birds do. Invite volunteers to guess how these penguins take care of their eggs. After several guesses have been made, explain that these penguins carry the eggs on their feet. Have each youngster stand with his feet close together and then place an egg on his feet. Invite him to waddle around the area while trying to keep the egg balanced on his feet. Encourage youngsters to discuss whether it is difficult to keep the eggs on their feet.

Cindy Hoying
Centerville, OH

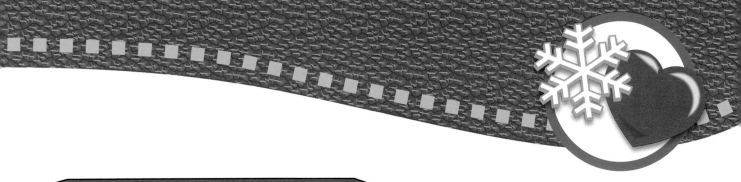

Penguin Places
Positional words

Penguins are here, there, and everywhere with this engaging activity. Place a copy of the penguin card on page 16 near your group-time area. Invite a volunteer to describe the penguin's location using positional words. After describing the location, have him move the penguin to a different place and call on a classmate to describe it. Continue in this manner until each child has had a turn.

Fishy Fun
Rhyming

Cut out a class supply of fish patterns (see page 18). Glue a copy of a picture card from page 18 to each fish. Place a blue sheet on the floor of your group-time area and scatter the fish on top of the sheet (water). In turn, have each student (penguin) waddle to the water and reach in to "catch" a fish. Have her name the picture on her fish. Then help her name a real or nonsense rhyming word.

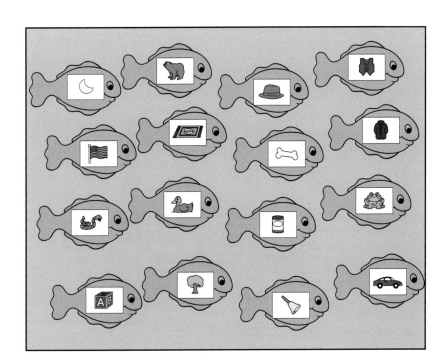

Group Time

Polar Bear Walk
Gross motor

Explain to youngsters that even though polar bears are large animals, they can walk on thin ice without breaking it. Tell them that polar bears place their paws far apart so their bodies are low to the ground. Then they carefully and quietly place each paw on the ice as they walk. Have youngsters crawl around the room as if they were polar bears attempting to walk on thin ice. Prompt them to move slowly and carefully with their bodies low to the ground.

Ada Goren
Winston-Salem, NC

Go for a Swim!
Making sets

Give each youngster in a small group ten cotton balls (polar bears) and a sheet of blue paper (water). Provide a stack of number cards. Invite each child to take a card and read the number. Then have her place that number of polar bears on the water. After checking students' work, have each child display her number card and lead the group in counting her swimming polar bears.

A Smile for Dr. King

Showing kindness to others

In advance, have each child make a double-sided puppet like the one shown. Discuss with youngsters that Dr. Martin Luther King Jr. wanted people to be kind to others. Announce a situation, such as "Cathy dropped her crayon box, and Jamie helped her pick up the crayons." Have each child hold up his puppet and display the happy face if the situation would make Dr. King happy. Have him display the sad face if the situation would make Dr. King sad. Continue with other situations, such as those suggested.

Suggested situations:
Sarah wouldn't share her crayons.
Jacob asked Lee to play.
Emma helped her mother make dinner.
Lincoln made fun of Amber's hair.
Jenna called a classmate names.
Juan asked Michael to play with him on the slide.

Join Hands!

Movement

Dr. Martin Luther King Jr. worked for many years encouraging people to be friendly toward each other. Explain that when people join hands, it shows that they are friendly. Challenge your little ones to see how quickly they can join hands with this fun activity! Have students stand in a circle with their arms at their sides. Start a stopwatch as you tap a child's shoulder. The child takes the hand of the classmate to her right. Youngsters continue in this manner until the last child takes the hand of the child who started the activity. Tell the group how long it took them to join hands. Invite them to repeat the activity, encouraging them to go faster for each subsequent round.

Ada Goren
Winston-Salem, NC

Group Time

Bag It!

To prepare, place an assortment of play foods or empty food packages in a basket, being sure to include some choices that are good for teeth and some that are not. Have youngsters sit in a circle around a paper grocery bag. Instruct youngsters to pass the basket around the circle as you lead the group in saying the rhyme shown. When the rhyme is finished, have the child with the basket take a food and show it to her classmates. If it is a food that is good for your teeth, have her put it in the grocery bag. If it is not good for your teeth, have her set it beside the bag. After all the foods have been used, lead youngsters in a discussion about why the foods in the bag are better for your teeth than the ones beside the bag.

Some foods make a healthy smile,
And some are not so great.
Choose a food and tell us—
Should it be on your plate?

Ada Goren
Winston-Salem, NC

Brush Away

Shape identification

Draw a large tooth outline on your whiteboard. Draw several different shapes (stains) inside the outline. Name a shape and then pass a soft bristle toothbrush to a child. Invite him to find a stain of that shape on the tooth and brush it away. Continue in this manner until no stains remain.

Ada Goren

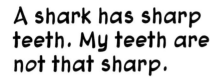

A shark has sharp teeth. My teeth are not that sharp.

All Kinds of Teeth

Making comparisons

Pass a mirror around the circle and invite each child to look at his teeth. Encourage students to describe what their teeth look like. Next, display several pictures of animal teeth. Encourage students to make observations about the animals' teeth. Then guide students to notice likenesses and differences between the teeth of animals and their own teeth.

Clare Cox
Homer Davis Elementary
Tucson, AZ

Shadow Search

Number recognition

Oh no! The groundhog's shadow is hiding, and your youngsters need to help the groundhog find it. Cut apart a copy of the shadow cards on page 19. Label the bottom of each of six paper plates (piles of snow) with a number from 1 to 6. Secretly place a shadow under each pile of snow. Invite a volunteer to name a number and look under the snow pile to determine whether the shadow hiding beneath it is the groundhog's. If it isn't, have him name the shape shadow. Continue in this manner until the groundhog's shadow is found. Rehide the shadows and play another round.

Roxanne LaBell Dearman
NC Early Intervention Program for Children Who Are Deaf or Hard of Hearing
Charlotte, NC

Group Time

I love you!

Special Delivery

Letter recognition

Label heart cutouts (valentines) with letters. Label a few extras with the phrase "I love you!" Then place the hearts in a tote bag. Invite a child to be the mail carrier. Have him walk around the circle, stop in front of a classmate, and deliver a valentine to her. If it has a letter on it, have her name the letter. If it has "I love you!" on it, have her blow kisses to her classmates. Invite the youngster who received the valentine to be the mail carrier. Continue until each child has delivered and received a valentine.

Cindy Hoying
Centerville, OH

Emma

Michael

Jenna

Mia

Whose Name?

Identifying one's name

Make a class supply of heart cutouts and write a different child's name on each one. To begin, recite the rhyme shown, holding up one of the hearts on the final line. When the child recognizes his name, give him his heart cutout to take home. Continue with each remaining heart cutout, prompting students to join in as you recite the rhyme each time.

A big heart, a little heart,
A heart that's red or blue,
A valentine heart
That's just for you!

Ada Goren
Winston-Salem, NC

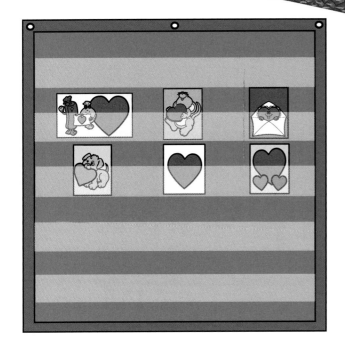

Shopping for Valentines

Using descriptive language

To set up a valentine store, place a collection of valentine cards in a pocket chart. In turn, invite a child to be the shopkeeper. Describe a valentine and then have her find the valentine and give it to you. Show the valentine to the class and ask them if it matches your description. If the valentine matches the description, have each child draw a heart in the air. If the valentine does not match the description, have them do nothing. Continue until each child has had a turn to be the shopkeeper.

Broken Hearts

Matching uppercase and lowercase letters

For this small-group game, write an uppercase and a lowercase letter pair on each of several heart cutouts and then puzzle-cut the hearts between the letters. Arrange the pieces so that they are facedown. In turn, invite each child to turn over two pieces. If the pieces match, she puts them together to make a whole heart and sets them aside. If the pieces don't match, she turns them back over. Continue in this manner until all the broken hearts are fixed.

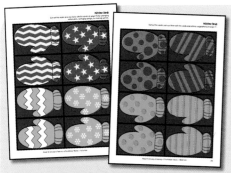

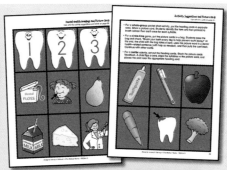

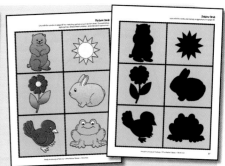

Check out the mitten cards on pages 71–73 for practice matching pairs!

Spotlight clapping syllables with the cards on pages 81–83!

Practice visual discrimination with the cards on pages 85–87.

Penguin Card

Use with "Penelope Penguin's Trip" on page 8 and "Penguin Places" on page 9.

Word Card and Picture Cards

Use with "Penelope Penguin's Trip" on page 8.

TEC61419

packs

TEC61419

TEC61419

POPCORN

TEC61419

Ready for January & February • ©The Mailbox® Books • TEC61419

TEC61419

TEC61419

TEC61419

TEC61419

TEC61419

TEC61419

Fish Patterns and Picture Cards
Use with "Fishy Fun" on page 9.

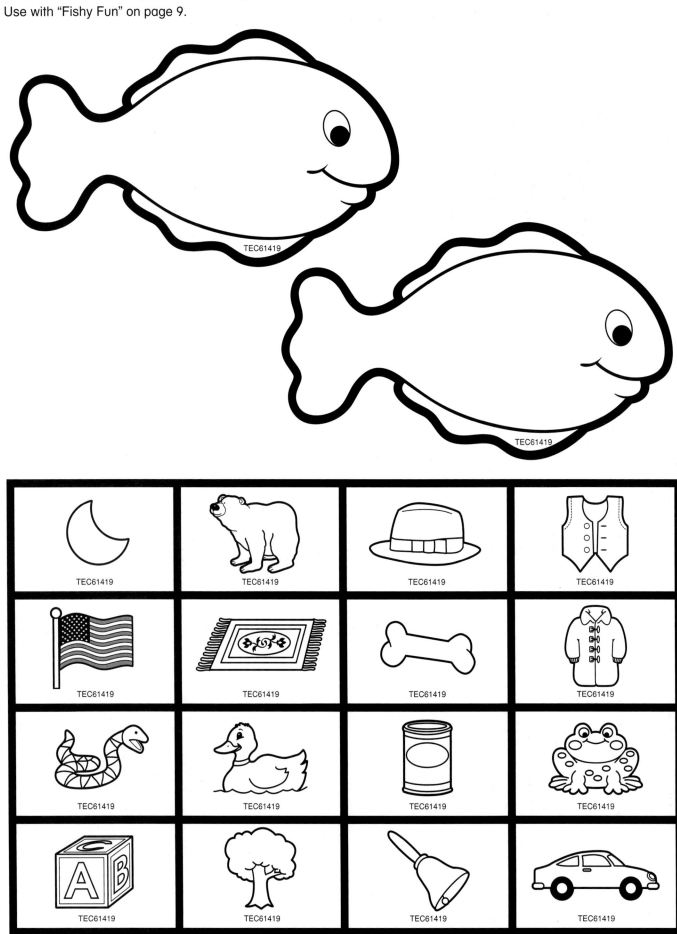

TEC61419

TEC61419

TEC61419

TEC61419

TEC61419

TEC61419

TEC61419

TEC61419

TEC61419

TEC61419

TEC61419

TEC61419

TEC61419

TEC61419

TEC61419

TEC61419

TEC61419

TEC61419

Ready for January & February • ©The Mailbox® Books • TEC61419

TEC61419

TEC61419

TEC61419

TEC61419

TEC61419

TEC61419

Songs & Such

When It's Midnight

Celebrate the New Year with this snappy tune and lots of noise! Hand out rhythm instruments or old-fashioned substitutes, like pots and pans, metal lids, and wood or plastic mixing spoons. Then lead youngsters in singing a round of the song with musical accompaniment!

(sung to the tune of "If You're Happy and You Know It")

When it's midnight and you know it, shout, "Happy New Year!"
When it's midnight and you know it, shout, "Happy New Year!"
When it's midnight and you know it, raise your voice and really show it.
When it's midnight and you know it, shout, "Happy New Year!"

Janet Boyce
Cokato, MN

Snow Is Falling

Youngsters create an indoor snowstorm with this wintry ditty! Give each child a craft foam snowflake (or white pom-pom). Then lead little ones in singing the song, prompting them to toss the snowflakes in the air at the end.

(sung to the tune of "Row, Row, Row Your Boat")

Snow is falling down,
Covering the ground.
Quietly, quietly, quietly, quietly
Snow is falling down!

Ada Goren
Winston-Salem, NC

I See Snow!

Is it a snowstorm or not? Youngsters decide after reciting this fun rhyme! As you lead little ones in saying the rhyme, gently float paper snowflakes to the ground when indicated. When the song ends, lead the group in counting the snowflakes. Then ask, "Was it a snowstorm or not?"

One little snowflake drifting about—
"I see snow!" I excitedly shout.
Another flake falls; now that makes two.
I hope it keeps snowing; yes, I do!
Two more flakes—that's three and four.
Down comes five, and then no more!

Tricia Kylene Brown
Bowling Green, KY

Cozy Hand Warmers

Lead your little ones in performing this fun rhyme about those wonderful winter hand warmers—mittens!

Mittens are just right for me.
They keep my hands warm as can be!
My fingers are hidden deep inside
With no place for my thumbs to hide!

Pretend to put on mittens.
Rub your hands together.
Curl your fingers to make fists.
Stick your thumbs up and wiggle them.

Ada Goren
Winston-Salem, NC

Songs & Such

Mitten Match

Students develop color-identification and matching skills with this simple song! Cut out pairs of colorful mittens, making sure that the pairs are different colors. Give each child a mitten. Choose a student and help him identify the color of his mitten. Then lead youngsters in singing the first verse of the song, inserting the child's name and mitten color. Prompt a student with the matching mitten to hold it in the air. Then sing the second verse, inserting the child's name and mitten color. Set the mittens aside and continue with other children and colors.

(sung to the tune of "Mary Had a Little Lamb")

[Child's name] has a [color] mitten,
[Color] mitten, [color] mitten.
[Child's name] has a [color] mitten.
Who has the other one?

[Child's name] has a [color] mitten,
[Color] mitten, [color] mitten.
[Child's name] has a [color] mitten.
Now we have a pair!

Tricia Kylene Brown
Bowling Green, KY

Penguins Are Cool!

Little ones will be eager to join in singing this cute penguin-themed song! Give each child a penguin cutout (patterns on page 29). Be sure to make one for yourself! Then lead youngsters in singing the song and manipulating the penguins.

(sung to the tune of "Three Blind Mice")

Black and white, black and white.
Penguins are black. Penguins are white.
They waddle around on the ice all day.
They swim, and they slide on their bellies to play.
They're birds that eat fish, but they can't fly away.
Penguins are cool!

Point to black and white on your penguin.
Point to black; point to white.
Waddle the penguin.
Slide the penguin.
Keep the penguin still.
Hold the penguin in the air.

Ada Goren
Winston-Salem, NC

Waddle, Waddle

Invite youngsters to show off their best penguin impersonations with this fun song! Place irregular-shaped white bulletin board paper (or a white bedsheet) on the floor so it resembles snow. Then invite your pint-size penguins to waddle around on the snow as you lead them in singing the song. During the final verse, prompt little ones to gently fall in the snow.

(sung to the tune of "Mary Had a Little Lamb")

> Waddle, waddle, penguin pals.
> Waddle fast; waddle slow.
> Waddle, waddle, penguin pals.
> [Waddle to and fro]!

Continue with the following: *Don't fall in the snow!*
Spoken—*Oops!*

Tricia Kylene Brown
Bowling Green, KY

It's Not Cold!

Cut out a copy of the arctic animal cards on page 48 and mount the cutouts on your board. Then use a snowflake pointer to highlight each animal as you lead students in reciting the rhyme shown.

"It's not cold!" says the polar bear.
"It's not cold!" says the seal.
"It's not cold!" says the walrus.
"We love how the arctic feels!"

"It's not cold!" says the caribou.
"It's not cold!" says the fox.
"It's not cold!" says the arctic hare.
"That's why we don't wear socks!"

Suzanne Moore
Tucson, AZ

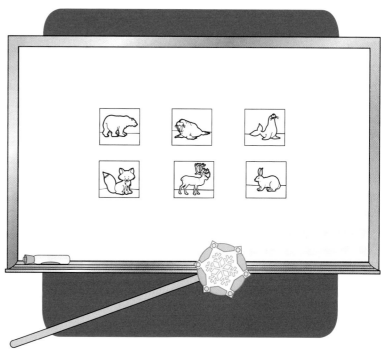

Songs & Such

Martin's Dream

Honor Dr. Martin Luther King Jr. and boost cooperation in your classroom with this easy-to-learn song!

(sung to the tune of "The Farmer in the Dell")

Oh, Martin Luther King,
Oh, Martin Luther King,
He dreamed of harmony
And peace for you and me!

He's George Washington!

Celebrate Presidents' Day with this fun sing-along about our nation's first president!

(sung to the tune of "Bingo")

There was a man who led the fight
For freedom in our country.
He's George Washington.
He's George Washington.
He's George Washington,
The father of our country!

Suzanne Moore
Tucson, AZ

Healthy and White

Teach little ones this melodic reminder to brush their teeth throughout the day.

(sung to the tune of "My Bonnie Lies Over the Ocean")

Please brush your teeth every morning.
Please brush your teeth every night.
Please brush your teeth after you've eaten
To keep your teeth healthy and white!

Brush them. Brush them.
Keep your teeth healthy and white, so white!
Brush them. Brush them.
Keep your teeth healthy and white!

Ada Goren
Winston-Salem, NC

B-R-U-S-H!

Remind little ones about good dental hygiene with this fun song! Write "BRUSH" on chart paper. Lead students in singing the song. Then sing and clap the song five more times, covering a letter with a tooth cutout each time and replacing that letter name with a clap as is done in the traditional song "Bingo."

(sung to the tune of "Bingo")

All little girls and boys I know
Should always brush their teeth–O.
B-R-U-S-H!
B-R-U-S-H!
B-R-U-S-H!
Should always brush their teeth–O!

Tricia Kylene Brown
Bowling Green, KY

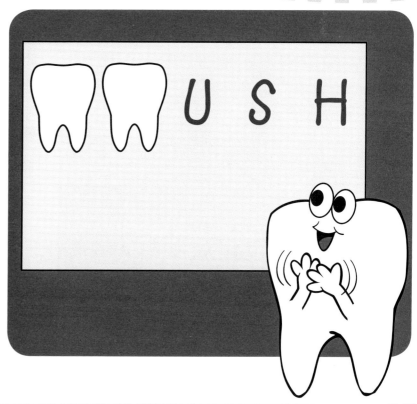

Songs & Such

What Is on My Teeth?

This zippy tune reminds youngsters to brush away bacteria to prevent tooth decay!

(sung to the tune of "The Farmer in the Dell")

Oh, what is on my teeth?
Oh, what is on my teeth?
Yucky bacteria—
That's what is on my teeth!

I brush it all away.
I brush it all away.
Goodbye, bacteria!
I won't have tooth decay!

Cindy Hoying
Centerville, OH

Mr. Groundhog

Here's a sweet tune that helps youngsters learn about the legend of the groundhog! Have little ones curl up on the floor, pretending to be groundhogs asleep in a burrow. Then sing the song, prompting your little groundhogs to wake up at the end and tell whether there will be six more weeks of winter or an early spring.

(sung to the tune of "Clementine")

Mr. Groundhog, sleepy groundhog,
Please wake up and take a peek.
If you see your little shadow,
Winter lasts for six more weeks.

Mr. Groundhog, sleepy groundhog,
Look around at everything.
If you do not see your shadow,
It will be an early spring!

Suzanne Moore
Tucson, AZ

Where Is Groundhog?

To prepare for this song and activity, place a groundhog cutout (pattern on page 49) somewhere in your classroom. Tell youngsters there's a groundhog somewhere in the room. Then have students join you in singing the song as you lead them on a groundhog search. After finding the groundhog, take it to a nearby window to decide if there will be six more weeks of winter or an early spring!

(sung to the tune of "Are You Sleeping?")

Where is Groundhog? Where is Groundhog?
Please wake up! Please come out!
No more hibernating! Please don't keep us waiting!
Tell us now—winter or spring?

Cindy Hoying
Centerville, OH

My Valentine Friend

Celebrate Valentine's Day with this sweet, easy-to-remember song!

(sung to the tune of "The Muffin Man")

Oh, will you be my valentine,
My valentine, my valentine?
Oh, will you be my valentine
And always be my friend?

Oh, yes, I'll be your valentine,
Your valentine, your valentine.
Yes, I'll be your valentine
And always be your friend.

Ada Goren
Winston-Salem, NC

Songs & Such

Heart to Heart

Make pairs of heart cutouts from patterned paper. Sort the hearts into two identical sets. Then give each child a heart from one set, keeping the second set for yourself. To begin, display a heart and sing the song, prompting the child with the matching heart to hold it in the air. After confirming a matching pair of hearts, set them aside and repeat the activity until all the hearts are matched.

(sung to the tune of "Mary Had a Little Lamb")

> Do you have a valentine,
> Valentine, valentine?
> Do you have a valentine
> That is a match to mine?

Tricia Kylene Brown
Bowling Green, KY

All Over the Place!

Teach youngsters this rhyme. Then encourage them to discuss what they have seen that indicates Valentine's Day is around the corner.

> Hearts with dots, hearts with stripes,
> Hearts with fancy lace,
> Heart-shaped boxes filled with candy
> All over the place!

Ada Goren
Winston-Salem, NC

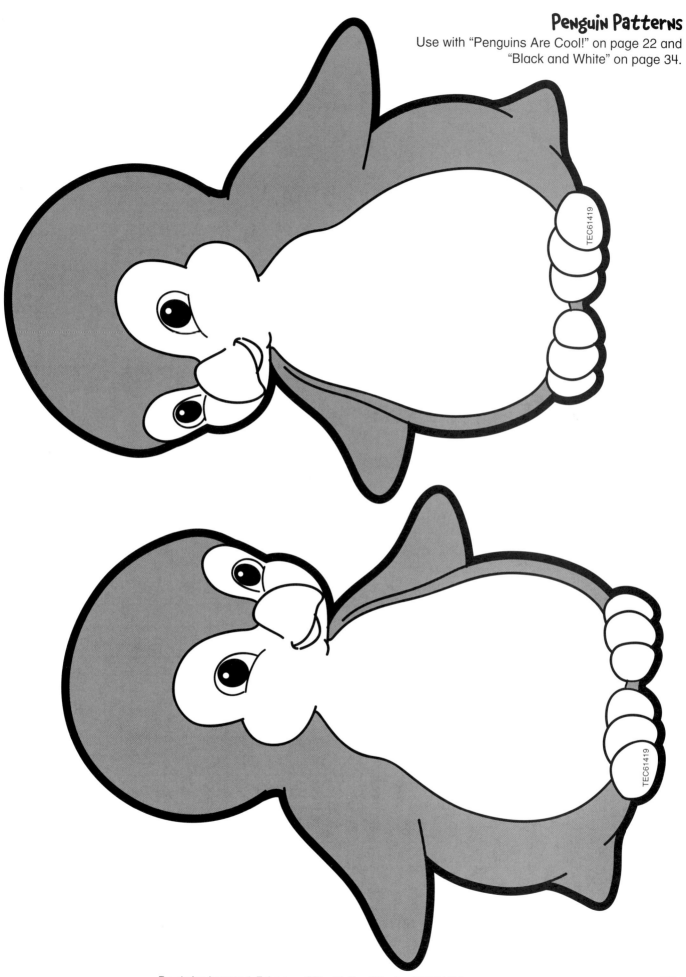

Centers

Literacy Center

Happy New Year!

Label 12 party hats with one letter each to spell *Happy New Year*. Arrange five hats to spell the word *Happy* and randomly set out the remaining hats. Display a banner labeled "Happy New Year" and provide musical instruments, such as a maraca and a tambourine. Using the banner as a guide, a youngster arranges the randomly placed hats to spell *New Year*. Then he says, "Happy New Year!" and concludes the activity with a musical celebration.
Recognizing letters, forming words

Games Center

New Calendar Year

Make several copies of the gameboard on page 45. Cut one copy apart to use as game cards and put them in a bag. Give each player a gameboard, 12 game markers, and a personalized party blower. In turn, students take a card from the bag and show the other players. Each child puts a marker on the matching square on his gameboard; then the card is set aside. For a New Year's twist, when the January space is marked, each player toots his party blower! Then that card is returned to the bag and used as a celebration prompt whenever it's pulled. Play continues until only the January card is left. ***Visual discrimination, participating in a game***

inspired by an idea from Tricia Kylene Brown
Bowling Green, KY

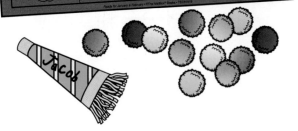

Snowy Landscape

Mix together in a plastic tub nonmentholated shaving cream, salt, and water until the mixture feels gritty and goopy; then sprinkle the mixture with iridescent glitter and add large white pom-poms to the tub. Provide plastic woodland animals and a small shovel or scoop. A youngster plays in the faux snow with the props. ***Exploring the senses***

adapted from an idea by Janet Boyce

Fine-Motor
Area

Snowman Stuffing

Place at a table clear, widemouthed plastic bottles with lids, white tissue paper, permanent markers, and an unsharpened pencil. A student stuffs a bottle with tissue paper, using the pencil to help push the tissue into the bottle. When he's finished, he screws on the lid and uses the markers to decorate the bottle with snowman details. ***Fine-motor skills***

Mary Robles
Portland, OR

Centers

How Many Snowballs?

On the inside of a sterilized egg carton, label ten sections with numbers 1 to 10. Provide a supply of small white pom-poms (snowballs). Close one snowball inside the carton and get a plastic pail. Place the items at a center. A child shakes the carton, tossing the snowball around inside. Then she opens the lid, identifies the number in the section the snowball has landed in, and puts that many snowballs in the pail. If the snowball lands in an unnumbered space, she closes the lid and tries again. She repeats the process until all the snowballs are in the pail. ***Number identification, counting***

Mary Robles
Portland, OR

Powerful Plow

Attach a length of heavy-duty tape (road) to the inside bottom of your sensory table. Use a permanent marker to add road details to the tape, if desired. Pour a generous amount of salt (snow) in the table to cover the road. Make a toy snowplow by taping a cardboard plow to the front of a toy truck (or simply provide a bulldozer toy to use as a snowplow). A youngster "drives" the plow through the snow, clearing the road for the cars. After clearing the road, he sprinkles snow from above the table to mimic another snowstorm. ***Fine-motor skills, pretend play***

Mary Robles

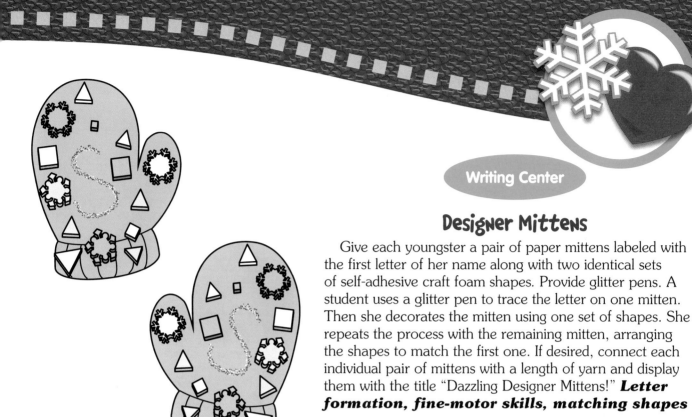

Designer Mittens

Give each youngster a pair of paper mittens labeled with the first letter of her name along with two identical sets of self-adhesive craft foam shapes. Provide glitter pens. A student uses a glitter pen to trace the letter on one mitten. Then she decorates the mitten using one set of shapes. She repeats the process with the remaining mitten, arranging the shapes to match the first one. If desired, connect each individual pair of mittens with a length of yarn and display them with the title "Dazzling Designer Mittens!" *Letter formation, fine-motor skills, matching shapes*

Roxanne LaBell Dearman
NC Early Intervention Program for Children Who Are Deaf or Hard of Hearing

Dramatic-Play Area

Chilly Treats Winter Café

Turn your dramatic-play area into a snow-laden ice cream café! Decorate the area with aluminum foil icicles, oversize snowbank cutouts, and cotton batting (snow). Provide an empty ice cream container filled with large pom-poms (ice cream scoops); an ice cream scooper; tagboard ice pops and ice cream cones; and winter-themed disposable bowls, cups, and napkins. Also provide a toy cash register, play money, and assorted outdoor winter wear. Youngsters use the props to engage in pretend ice cream café play with a wintry twist! *Role-playing*

adapted from an idea by Deborah J. Ryan
Beaverton, OR

Centers

Black and White

Enlarge the penguin patterns on page 29 and then copy them to make a class supply. Place the penguins at a center along with a tub filled with a variety of black and white craft supplies, such as pom-poms, tissue paper squares, craft foam pieces, yarn, fabric, and construction paper scraps. A child colors a penguin and then chooses craft items, feeling their texture as he does so. Then he glues the items on and around his penguin. **Exploring the sense of touch**

Play Dough Center

Stony Nest

Share with youngsters that a chinstrap penguin usually builds a nest using just enough stones to keep its eggs from rolling away. Then place at a table a batch of gray play dough and several white plastic eggs. A child molds chunks of play dough so they resemble stones; then she arranges the stones to form a nest. When she's finished, she places eggs in the nest to see if her construction keeps them from rolling away. **Fine-motor skills**

Cindy Hoying
Centerville, OH

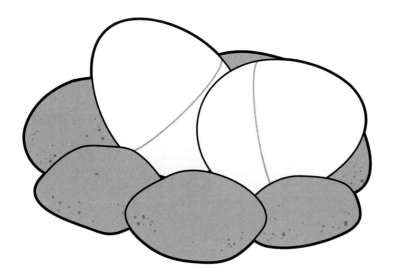

Tip the Iceberg

Use a permanent marker to transform several table tennis balls into penguin look-alikes. Float the penguins in your water table (ocean) along with a white plastic plate (iceberg). Provide a pair of tongs. A youngster uses the tongs to pick up each penguin and place it on the iceberg. Then she tips the iceberg and slides the penguins back into the ocean! ***Fine-motor skills***

Tricia Kylene Brown
Bowling Green, KY

Math Center

Penguins Aplenty!

For this partner center, provide two iceberg cutouts and 19 black pom-poms (penguins). Place number cards from 1 to 10 in a bag. Add corresponding dot sets to the cards, if desired. Each child takes a card from the bag and counts to place the corresponding number of penguins on his iceberg. When youngsters are finished, they compare the number of penguins to see which iceberg has *more* and which has *fewer*. ***Number recognition, counting, comparing numbers***

Cindy Hoying
Centerville, OH

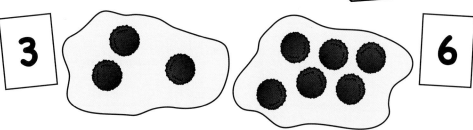

Centers

Block Center

Tall as a Polar Bear

When measured on all fours, the heights of most adult polar bears are typically from 3.5 to five feet for both males and females. With this fact in mind, cut a life-size polar bear shape from white bulletin board paper and attach it to your wall. Provide enough same-size rectangular blocks to match the bear's height when they are stacked. A child stacks the blocks as tall as the bear and then counts to see how many blocks tall the bear is.
Nonstandard measurement

Ada Goren
Winston-Salem, NC

Literacy Center

P Is for Pawprint!

For this partner game, cut out a copy of the cards on page 46 and put the cutouts in a bag. Place the bag at a center along with a copy of the gameboard on page 47. Each youngster places a white pom-pom (polar bear) on a different start space. In turn, each child takes a card from the bag. When a card shows a *P*, he moves his bear forward one pawprint. When it shows a different letter, he keeps the bear on the current space and his turn ends. When the pawprint card is picked, he moves the bear back one space. The card is returned to the bag, and play continues until each polar bear reaches the ocean.
Recognizing letters

Build a Bear

For this yummy polar bear snack, give each child one-half of a sandwich round (head), one banana slice cut in half (ears), two black olive slices (eyes), and one-half of a purple seedless grape (nose). Also provide whipped cream cheese, paper plates, and plastic knives. A child puts the sandwich round on a plate and uses a knife to spread cream cheese on the round. She adds the ears, eyes, and nose to complete her bear and then enjoys her snack! *Fine-motor skills*

Science Center

Tundra Twins

Cut out two copies of the arctic animal cards on page 48. Arrange one set of cards on a tray and hide the remaining set in your sensory table amid white paper shreds or packing peanuts (snow). A youngster searches through the snow and finds an animal card. He identifies the animal, with help as needed. Then he places it on the tray with the matching card. He continues until all the arctic animals are paired. *Investigating living things, visual discrimination*

Ada Goren
Winston-Salem, NC

Centers

Working Together

For this partner center, make two printouts of a picture of Martin Luther King Jr. (an Internet image search will turn up many options). Attach one picture to a manila envelope labeled with his name and the remaining picture to a sheet of tagboard. Puzzle-cut the tagboard picture into several pieces; then place the resulting puzzle and the envelope at a center. Two youngsters visit the center and work together to assemble the puzzle, referring to the picture as needed. When the puzzle is complete, the youngsters shake hands and say, "Working together is lots of fun. It helped us get this puzzle done!" Then they disassemble the puzzle. When center time is over, store the puzzle pieces in the envelope. **Social skills**

Play Dough Center

Peace and Love

Here's a perfect activity to follow up a discussion about Martin Luther King Jr.'s dream of peace and love! Use a permanent marker to draw a large peace sign on a vinyl placemat. Put the placemat at a table along with play dough. A child rolls play dough into ropes and arranges it on the placemat to form a three-dimensional peace sign. **Fine-motor skills**

Ada Goren
Winston-Salem, NC

Delightful Dentistry

Place on a tray an empty dental floss container, a new toothbrush, a toothpaste box, a disposable "rinse" cup, and a small hand mirror. Also provide an oversize white button-down shirt (lab coat), personalized surgical masks, latex-free disposable gloves, a doll (patient), and a toy high chair (dentist chair). A youngster uses the props to engage in pretend dental office play. **Role-playing**

Math Center

How Many Teeth?

Draw a simple head on a sheet of paper, making sure the head has a large open mouth. Provide white linking cubes (teeth) and a large foam die. A child rolls the die and counts the dots. Then she places the appropriate number of teeth on the mouth. She continues until the mouth is filled with lots of teeth! **For a partner game,** make two heads on separate sheets of paper. Then have each student roll the die, in turn, and then place the appropriate number of teeth on her drawing. Students compare the sets, remove the teeth, and play another round. ***Counting, comparing sets***

Norinne Weeks
Carrillo Elementary
Houston, TX

Centers

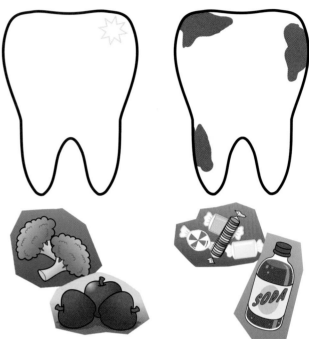

Health Center

Good for Your Teeth or Not?

For this teacher-guided center, display a plain white tooth cutout and one with markings to represent plaque and tartar. Cut out magazine pictures of food and drink items that are healthy and not so healthy for teeth and place them in a bag. Have a student take a picture from the bag and identify the item; then encourage her to tell whether it's healthy or not so healthy for teeth and why. After confirming a correct response, prompt her to place the picture near the appropriate tooth. Repeat the process until the bag is empty. **Sorting**

Fine-Motor Area

Floss and Brush

Cut the bottom from a clear plastic drink bottle and recycle the top portion. Stuff the bottle bottom with cotton; then hot-glue it to a piece of cardboard, as shown, to create a model tooth. Place the tooth at a table with a length of white yarn, a new toothbrush, and a tube of toothpaste with the lid secured in place. A youngster uses the yarn to floss the tooth. Then he pretends to squeeze toothpaste onto the toothbrush and brushes the tooth. **Fine-motor skills**

Tricia Kylene Brown
Bowling Green, KY

Sand Table

Groundhog's Habitat

Place small and large cardboard tubes at your sand table. Provide books on groundhogs. Before youngsters visit the center, help them understand that groundhogs live in burrows under the ground. A child visits the center and looks at the books. Then she uses the tubes to make groundhog burrows beneath the sand. *Investigating living things*

Cindy Hoying, Centerville, OH

Science Center

Look! A Shadow!

In advance, take youngsters outside on a sunny day and have them notice their shadows and where the shadows are in relation to the sun. Provide groundhog cutouts (see the pattern on page 49), sheets of construction paper, and black paper scraps. A child colors a groundhog and glues it to a sheet of paper. Then she draws a sun on the paper. Next, she tears strips of paper and glues them to show where the groundhog's shadow would be. *Exploring shadows*

Centers

Math Center

Chock-Full o' Chocolates!

Display ten brown pom-poms (chocolates) in a heart-shaped candy box. From a deck of playing cards, stack facedown all the number cards from the suit of hearts. A youngster flips the top card and identifies the number (or counts the large hearts to help identify the number). She takes that many chocolates from the box, counting each one as she works; then she counts the remaining chocolates in the box to see how many are left. She returns the chocolates to the box and repeats the process with each remaining card. ***Identifying numbers, counting, presubtraction skills***

Janet Boyce
Cokato, MN

Literacy Center

Hugs and Kisses

Fill a plastic tub with a mixture of dry rice and valentine-related confetti. Hide in the tub a collection of X and O letter tiles (or squares of craft foam labeled with Xs and Os). Provide a slotted spoon and two gift bags labeled as shown. A student uses the spoon to retrieve the hidden tiles and deposit each one he finds in the appropriate bag. Each time he deposits an X, he blows a kiss; for an O, he hugs himself! ***Sorting letters***

Janet Boyce

Writing Center

Secret Valentine Pal

For each child, write a valentine greeting and her name on the front of a construction paper card. Put the cards in a bag and place the bag at a table with valentine-themed stickers and glitter markers. Have each student visit the center and randomly take a card from the bag, returning it for a different one if she takes her own. She decorates the card and dictates a valentine message for an adult helper to write; then she signs the card and places it in a collection bin. After all the cards are collected, each child gives the one she decorated to her "Secret Valentine Pal." ***Fine-motor skills***

Ada Goren
Winston-Salem, NC

Literacy Center

Hanging Hearts

Label 26 die-cut hearts with letters from *A* to *Z*. Suspend a mock clothesline in a safe area; then clip most of the hearts to the line in alphabetical order, leaving space where needed to add the remaining hearts. Scatter the loose hearts faceup and provide a container of clothespins. Display an alphabet strip nearby. A child reads the displayed letters in alphabetical order, pausing at an empty space to name the missing letter. Then he finds the heart with the appropriate letter and clips it in place. He repeats the process until all the hearts are hung in alphabetical order. ***Alphabetical order***

Ada Goren

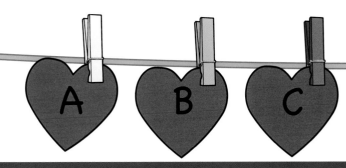

Centers

Play Dough Center

Pretty Patterns

Provide play dough in two valentine-related colors. Also provide a rolling pin, a heart-shaped cookie cutter, and a pattern strip like the one shown. A child studies the strip and then reads the pattern aloud. Then she uses the play dough and props to make the corresponding-color hearts, placing each heart below the strip as she works. Finally, she reads the play dough pattern aloud. **For an added challenge**, provide play dough in three colors and an *ABC* pattern strip. ***Patterning***

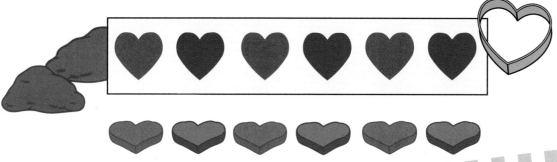

Gross-Motor Area

Hopscotch Hearts

Attach large heart cutouts to the floor in a hopscotch-style pattern, as shown. A child hops along the hearts, landing on one foot for a single heart and two feet for double hearts. When he reaches the end of the hearts, he turns around and repeats the process. ***Hopping***

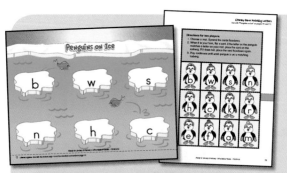

Check out the mats and cards on pages 75–79 for practice matching letters.

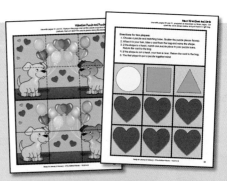

Spotlight shapes with the puzzle center on pages 89–93!

Practice writing with the story starter on page 95.

A New Calendar Year!

January	February	March	April
May	June	July	August
September	October	November	December

Note to the teacher: Use with "New Calendar Year" on page 30.

Game Cards

Use with "*P* Is for *Pawprint*!" on page 36.

P

TEC61419

P

TEC61419

P

TEC61419

S

TEC61419

N

TEC61419

Go **back**
1 pawprint.

TEC61419

Ready for January & February • ©The Mailbox® Books • TEC61419

P Is for Pawprint!

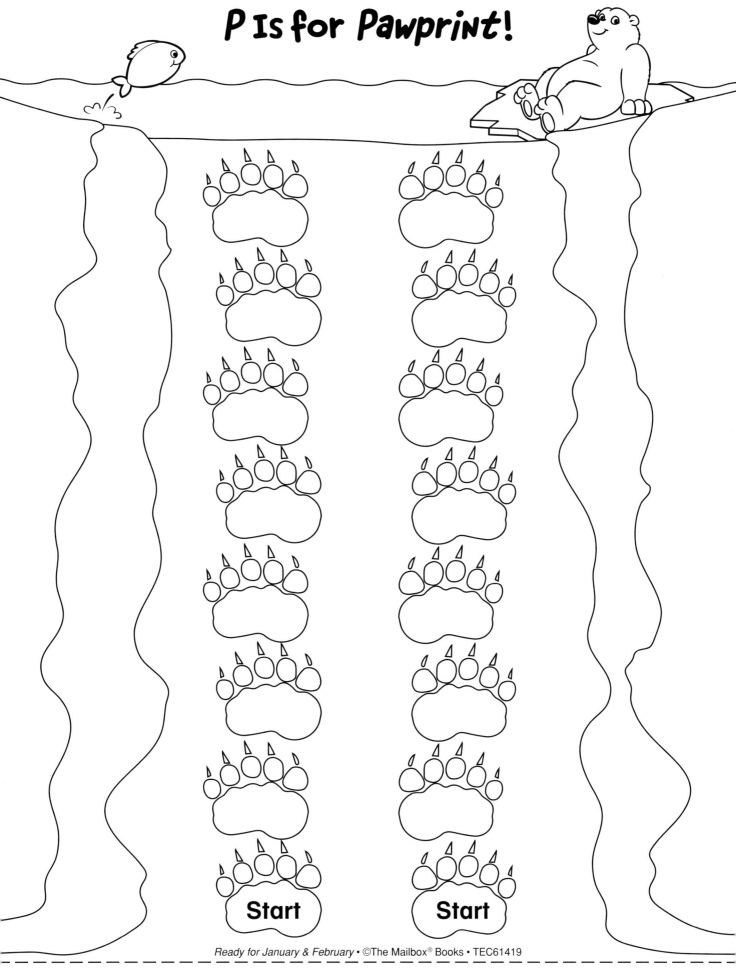

Start   **Start**

Arctic Animal Cards
Use with "It's Not Cold!" on page 23 and "Tundra Twins" on page 37.

TEC61419

TEC61419

TEC61419

TEC61419

TEC61419

TEC61419

Use with "Where Is Groundhog?" on page 27 and "Look! A Shadow!" on page 41.

TEC61419

Arts & Crafts

New Year's Fireworks

Create a New Year's fireworks display in your classroom with these projects. Place colorful star-shaped foil stickers on a sheet of black paper, being sure to leave plenty of space around each star. Then use colored chalk to draw lines out from each star. Lightly mist the project with hair spray and set it aside to dry.

Janet Boyce
Cokato, MN

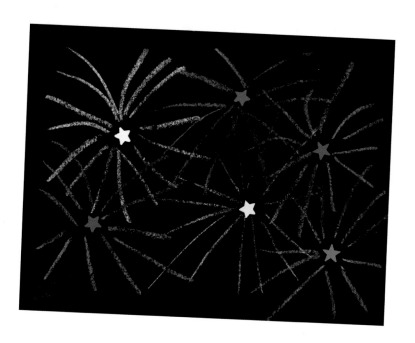

Process Art

Celebrate With Confetti

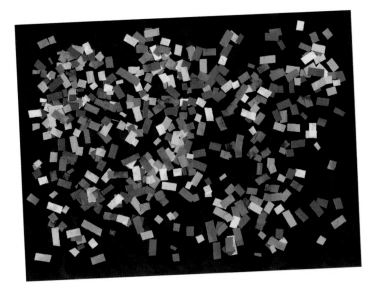

To make confetti, cut thin strips of colorful paper into small pieces over a paper plate. Continue cutting until you have made a large amount of confetti. Lay a sheet of black construction paper inside a box lid. Squeeze gel glue on the black paper in a design of your choice. Then toss pinches of confetti into the air above the box as you exclaim, "Happy New Year!" Continue in this manner until a desired effect is reached. Remove the paper from the box and set it aside to dry.

Janet Boyce

Fluffy Snowman

Get a paper plate. Place a dollop of nonmentholated shaving cream, a large puddle of glue, and white paper shreds on the plate. Use your hands to mix the items on the plate until a goopy mixture is formed. Then spread the mixture on a snowman cutout (pattern on page 61) until the snowman is evenly covered. Cut or tear facial details and accessories from scrap paper and then press them on the snowman.

Mary Robles
Portland, OR

Covered With Snow!

Color and cut out a copy of the house, tree, and truck patterns on page 62. Glue the cutouts to a sheet of light blue construction paper. Then use glue to outline the sides and top of each cutout. Next, tear or stretch cotton balls and place the cotton on the glue so that it looks like snow has fallen on the object. If desired, add some cotton around the objects so it looks like snow on the ground.

Janet Boyce
Cokato, MN

Arts & Crafts

Footprints in the Snow

Remove your shoes and place them on a sheet of gray construction paper. Trace the shoes and then put them back on your feet. Brush a mixture of equal parts white paint and glue around the tracings. To give the project a little sparkle, sprinkle salt on the painted area and shake off any excess. After the projects are dry, display them on a board titled "Footprints in the Snow."

Janet Boyce
Cokato, MN

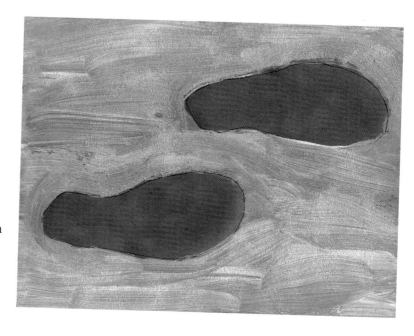

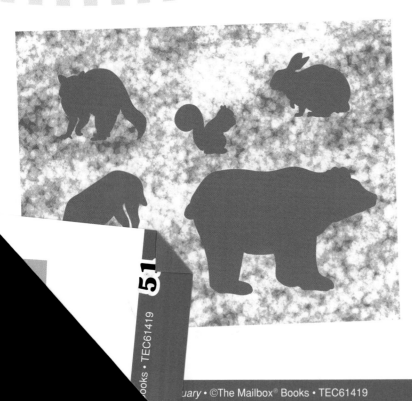

Snowy Critters

Lightly tape a few animal die-cuts onto a sheet of dark construction paper. Place the paper on a protected surface. Then spray thinned white tempera paint over the entire surface of the paper. After the paint is dry, remove the cutouts to reveal the shapes of the animals.

Marvelous Mittens

Rub an unwrapped flesh-tone crayon in the middle of a paper plate. Then add facial features so they resemble your own. Choose an unwrapped crayon in your favorite color and rub it around the edge of the plate so it looks like a hood. Draw designs on a pair of mitten cutouts and then stretch out cotton balls and glue them to the mittens so they resemble cuffs. To complete the project, glue the mittens to the hooded face as shown.

Janet Boyce
Cokato, MN

A Cool Bird

No study of penguins is complete without learning about the macaroni penguin. Use black paint to paint a paper plate half. After the paint is dry, attach two hole reinforcers (eyes) and a beak cutout. To make the penguin's crest of feathers, fold a 1" x 9" strip of yellow paper in half and make cuts toward the fold, being sure to stop before the fold. Unfold the strip and refold it so it resembles a V. Then glue the strip to the back of the penguin's head.

Janet Boyce

Arts & Crafts

Penguin Pals

Dip a triangular cosmetic sponge into a shallow container of black paint and make several prints (penguin bodies) on a sheet of construction paper. Then dip a pointer finger in the black paint and make a print at the top of each triangular print so it looks like the penguin's head. After using a wipe to clean your pointer finger, dip a pinkie finger in the orange paint and make prints on each penguin so they look like beaks and feet. Finally, add a white fingerprint belly to each penguin.

Janet Boyce, Cokato, MN

Dive Time

To make a penguin body, use a white crayon to trace your shoe onto black construction paper. Cut out the tracing and draw an eye and a white belly on the penguin. Glue three orange triangles (beak and feet) to the penguin as shown. Then glue a black semicircle (wing) to the penguin. (If desired, only glue a portion of the wing in place. Then bend the remaining portion outward to give the project dimension.) Glue the finished penguin to a sheet of blue paper. Next, tear pieces of waxed paper and attach them to the project so they resemble chunks of ice. Finally, use a blue crayon to add bubbles to the project.

Janet Boyce

54

Process Art

A Furry Friend

To make one of these adorable polar bears, dip a scrub brush with soft bristles into a shallow container of white paint. Paint with the brush on a large sheet of black construction paper, leaving only the *edges* of the paper unpainted. Then use black paint to paint the ears, eyes, and a muzzle near the top of the paper.

Janet Boyce
Cokato, MN

Torn Paper Polar Bear

Tear a large scrap of white paper so it resembles a large ice block and glue it to a sheet of blue construction paper. To make the polar bear's body, arrange a 5½" x 8½" piece of paper vertically. Then round the top two corners. Beginning at the bottom of the paper, tear a section away so the remaining paper resembles a horseshoe shape (body). Tear a polar bear head and ears from the scrap removed in the last step. Glue the body, head, and ears to the construction paper. Then add details as desired.

Arts & Crafts

Seals in the Snow

Dip a bath pouf in a shallow container of white paint. Press the pouf on a sheet of blue construction paper and twist it back and forth a couple of times before picking it up. Repeat the process two more times. To make seals, glue black paper eyes and black pom-pom noses to the prints. Then draw whiskers. Tear or stretch cotton balls and glue them around the seals so it looks like they are lying in the snow.

A Peace Quilt

Martin Luther King Jr. spent many years of his life encouraging people to live together peacefully. Decorate a copy of the peace sign pattern on page 63 as desired and then cut it out. Glue the peace sign to a colorful nine-inch paper square. Display the finished squares together so they resemble a quilt.

Janet Boyce
Cokato, MN

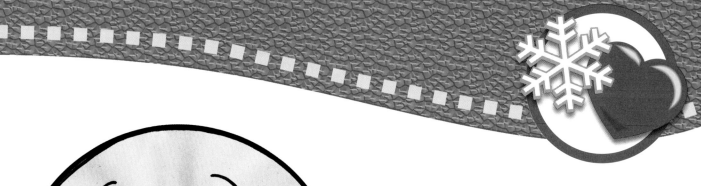

Big Smiles

Spotlight dental health with this simple project! To make one, use a black marker to draw a face, similar to the one shown, on an eight-inch yellow construction paper circle. Then dip a pointer finger in a shallow container of white paint and make prints (teeth) around the inner edge of the grin.

Janet Boyce
Cokato, MN

Toothbrush Tap

Place small amounts of colorful paint on a paper plate. Dip the bristles of a clean toothbrush in one of the paints and then gently tap it on a sheet of white construction paper. Pick up more paint as needed. Repeat the process with the other colors until a desired effect is reached.

Janet Boyce

Arts & Crafts

The Tooth Fairy

To mark where the tooth fairy's wings should be placed, put a cutout copy of the tooth pattern from page 64 on a sheet of paper and make a small pencil mark on either side of the tooth. Remove the tooth. Press your hands in a shallow container of pink paint and then press them on the paper so the inner edge of the hands overlaps the pencil marks. Next, decorate the large tooth cutout so it resembles a tooth fairy. Glue the tooth fairy to the paper as shown. To complete the project, add desired details such as a wand.

Janet Boyce
Cokato, MN

A Lovely Groundhog!

Make two heart cutouts in different sizes. Sponge-paint the hearts with brown paint. When the paint is dry, attach the hearts to a sheet of paper as shown. Then use a black marker to draw facial features, ears, and paws. Finally, use crayons to add burrow and tree details.

Janet Boyce

Out of the Burrow

To make this cute groundhog, round the corners of a 4" x 6" brown paper rectangle and then use crayons to add facial details and paws. Next, fold a paper plate in half. Unfold it and cut a slit along the fold line in the center of the plate. Color one half of the center section black (the groundhog's shadow). Color the rest of the plate brown. Slide the groundhog through the slit in the paper plate so that half of its body is showing.

Janet Boyce
Cokato, MN

Valentine Chocolates

Glue a brown heart cutout (liner) to a slightly larger red heart cutout (candy box). To make candy wrappers, use decorative scissors to cut strips from a paper lunch bag into smaller pieces. Glue the wrappers to the liner. Then dip a thumb in brown paint and make a thumbprint candy on each wrapper.

Janet Boyce

Arts & Crafts

Talking Hearts

On a sheet of light-colored construction paper, make several heart tracings. Then use colored chalk to color in the tracings. Lightly spray your paper with hair spray and set it aside to dry for a few minutes. Then use markers to write a message on each heart, with help as needed. (Tip: post a list of simple messages youngsters can refer to as they write on the hearts.)

Janet Boyce
Cokato, MN

Process Art

Hearts and Flowers

Dip a heart-shaped cookie cutter in a shallow container of red paint and make a few prints on a sheet of purple construction paper. Then dip a gift bow in the red paint and make a few more prints. Repeat the process using white and pink paint until a desired effect is reached.

Janet Boyce

TEC61419

House, Evergreen Tree, and Truck Patterns

Use with "Covered With Snow!" on page 51.

TEC61419

TEC61419

TEC61419

Peace Symbol Pattern
Use with "A Peace Quilt" on page 56.

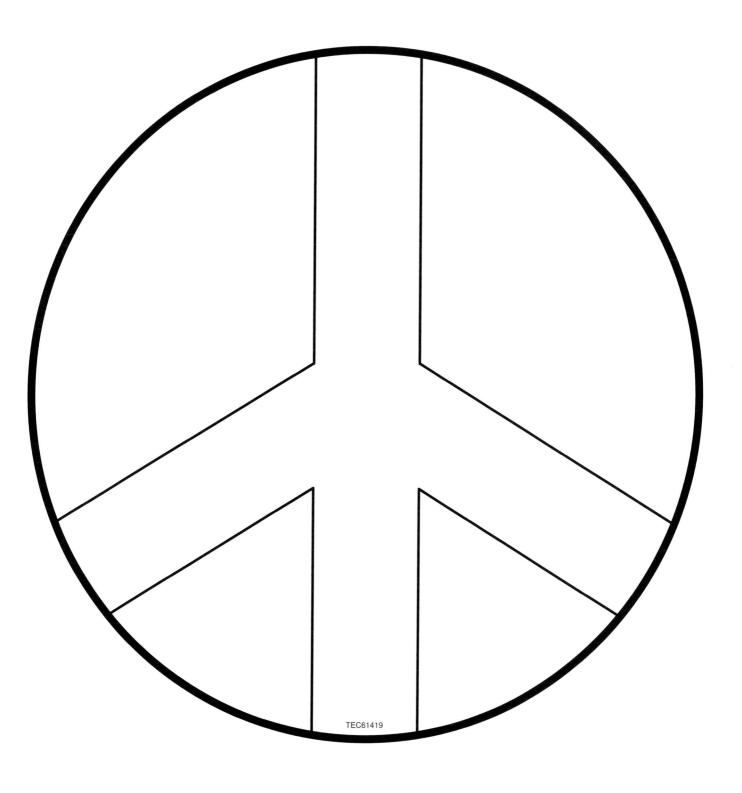

TEC61419

Tooth Pattern

Use with "The Tooth Fairy" on page 58.

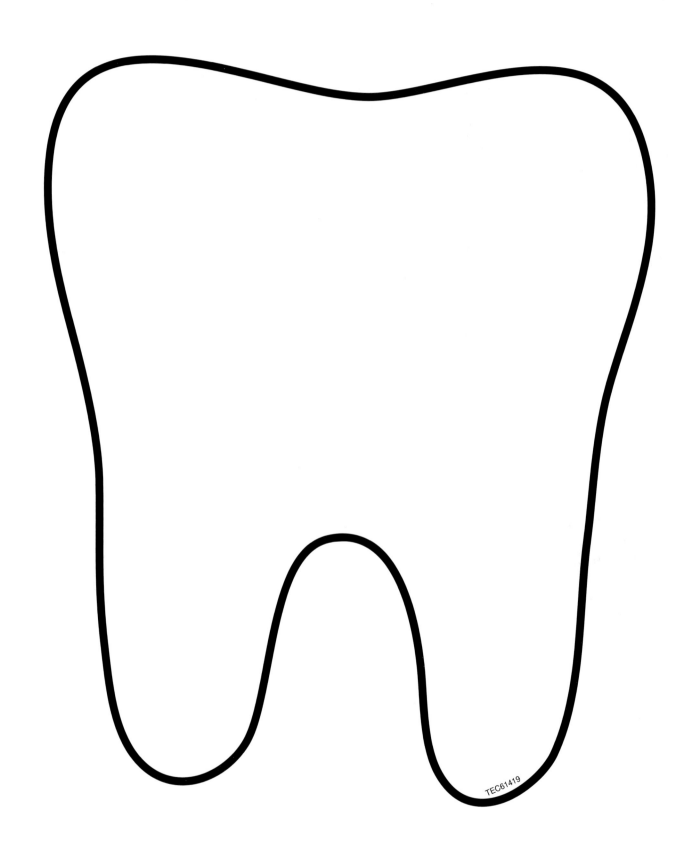

TEC61419

Literacy game: Remove this page and put it in a plastic page protector for durability. Use with pages 67 and 69.

Literacy Game
TEC61419

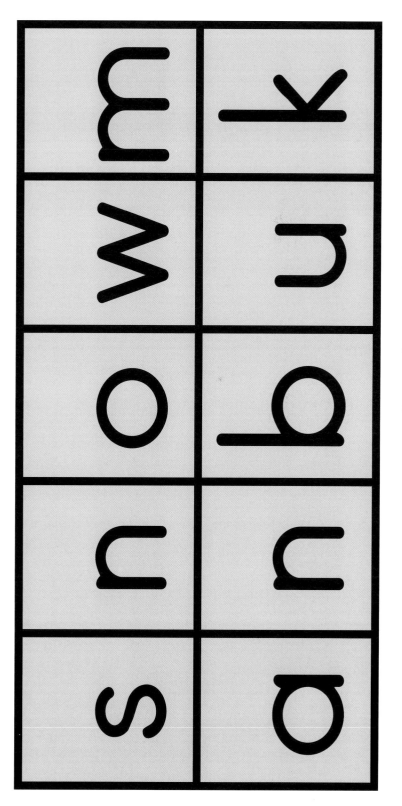

Literacy Game
TEC61419

Literacy Game
TEC61419

Literacy Game
TEC61419

Literacy Game
TEC61419

Literacy Game
TEC61419

Literacy Game
TEC61419

Literacy Game
TEC61419

Literacy Game
TEC61419

Literacy Game
TEC61419

Literacy Game
TEC61419

Directions:

1. Cut out the accessories below and the word strip and letter cards on page 67. Laminate them for sturdiness and durability.
2. Display the mat from page 65 and the word strip in a pocket chart. Set out the accessories. Put the cards in a bag.
3. A child takes a card from the bag. If the letter shown is in the word *snowman,* he places the card below the matching letter on the strip and adds one snowman accessory. If it is not, he returns the card to the bag and his turn is over. No accessory is added.
4. Play continues, in turn, until the word *snowman* is complete and the accessories are in place.

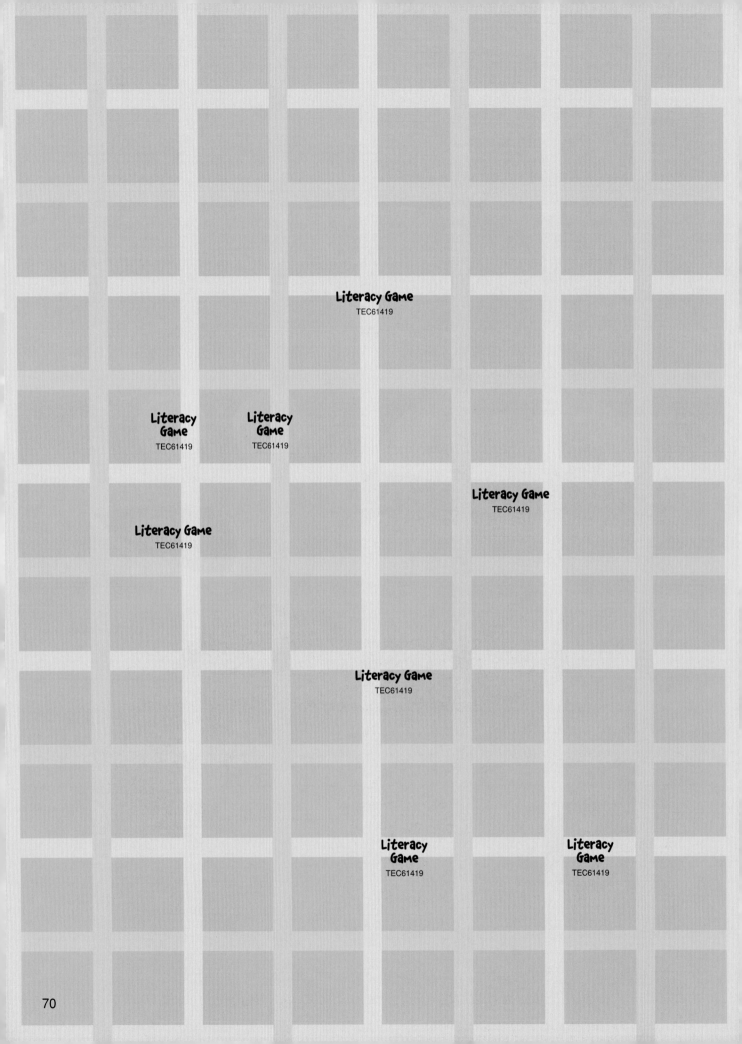

Literacy Game
TEC61419

Literacy
Game
TEC61419

Literacy
Game
TEC61419

Literacy Game
TEC61419

Literacy Game
TEC61419

Literacy Game
TEC61419

Literacy Game
TEC61419

Literacy
Game
TEC61419

Literacy
Game
TEC61419

Mitten Cards

Cut out the cards and use them with the cards on page 73 for arranging mitten pairs, sorting by design, or memory games.

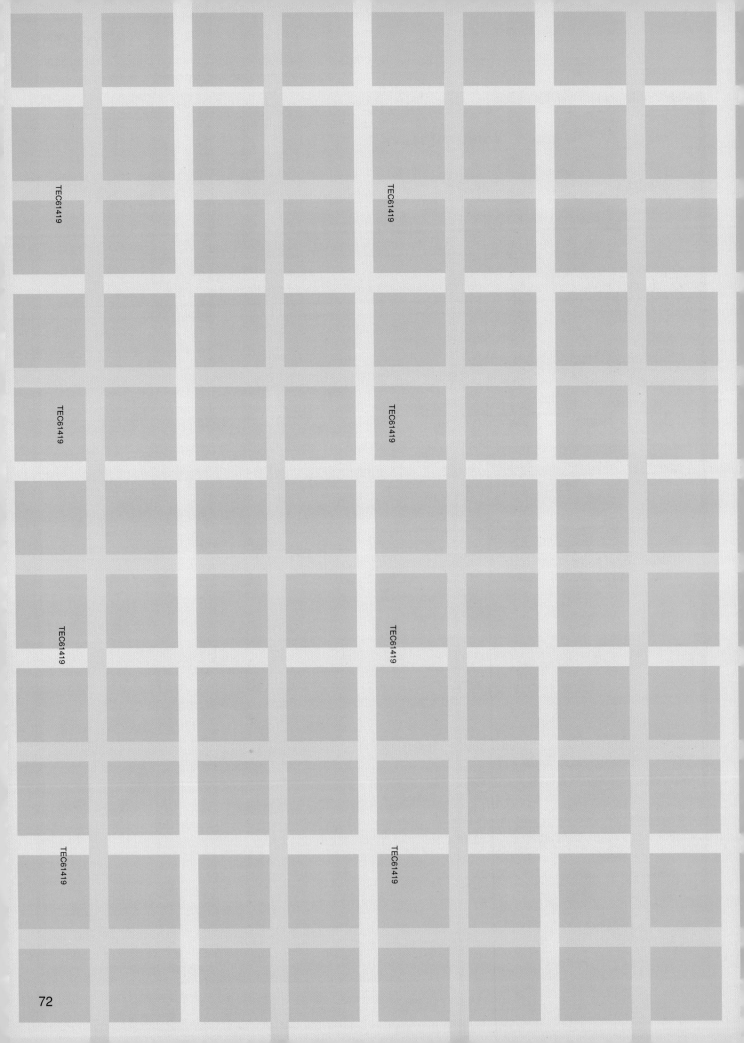

TEC61419

TEC61419

TEC61419

TEC61419

TEC61419

TEC61419

TEC61419

TEC61419

Cut out the cards and use them with the cards and activity suggestions on page 71.

Penguins on Ice

e

m

r

a

k

f

Ready for January & February • ©The Mailbox® Books • TEC61419

Literacy game: Use with the mat on page 77 and the directions and cards on page 79.

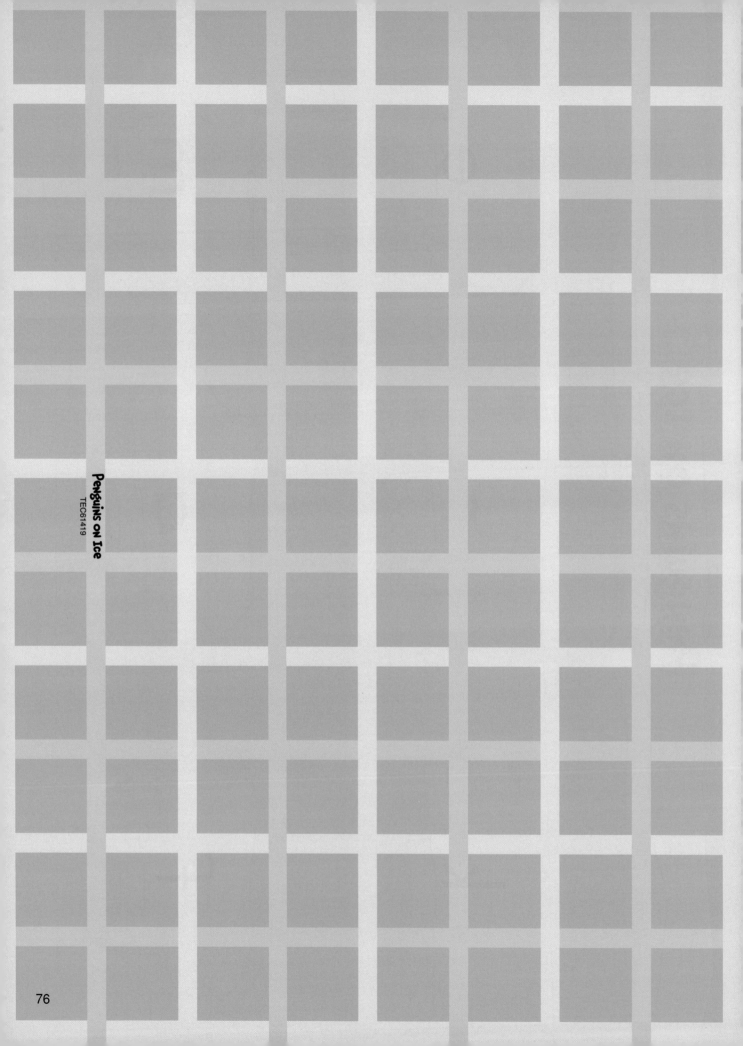

Penguins on Ice
TEC61419

Penguins on Ice

s

c

w

h

b

n

Ready for January & February • ©The Mailbox® Books • TEC61419

Literacy game: Use with the mat on page 75 and the directions and cards on page 79.

Penguins on Ice
TEC61419

Directions for two players:

1. Choose a mat. Spread the cards facedown.
2. When it is your turn, flip a card. If the letter on the penguin matches a letter on your mat, place the card on the iceberg. If it does not, place the card facedown again.
3. Play continues until each penguin is on a matching iceberg.

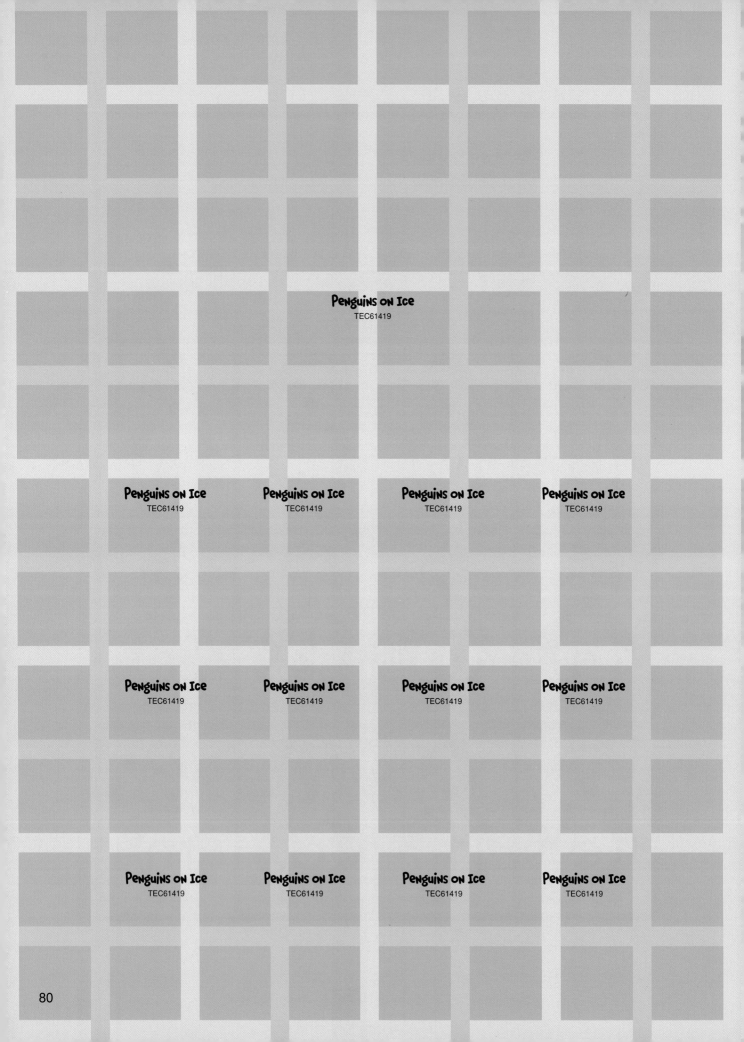

Penguins on Ice
TEC61419

Penguins on Ice
TEC61419

Penguins on Ice
TEC61419

Penguins on Ice
TEC61419

Penguins on Ice
TEC61419

Penguins on Ice
TEC61419

Penguins on Ice
TEC61419

Penguins on Ice
TEC61419

Penguins on Ice
TEC61419

Penguins on Ice
TEC61419

Penguins on Ice
TEC61419

Penguins on Ice
TEC61419

Penguins on Ice
TEC61419

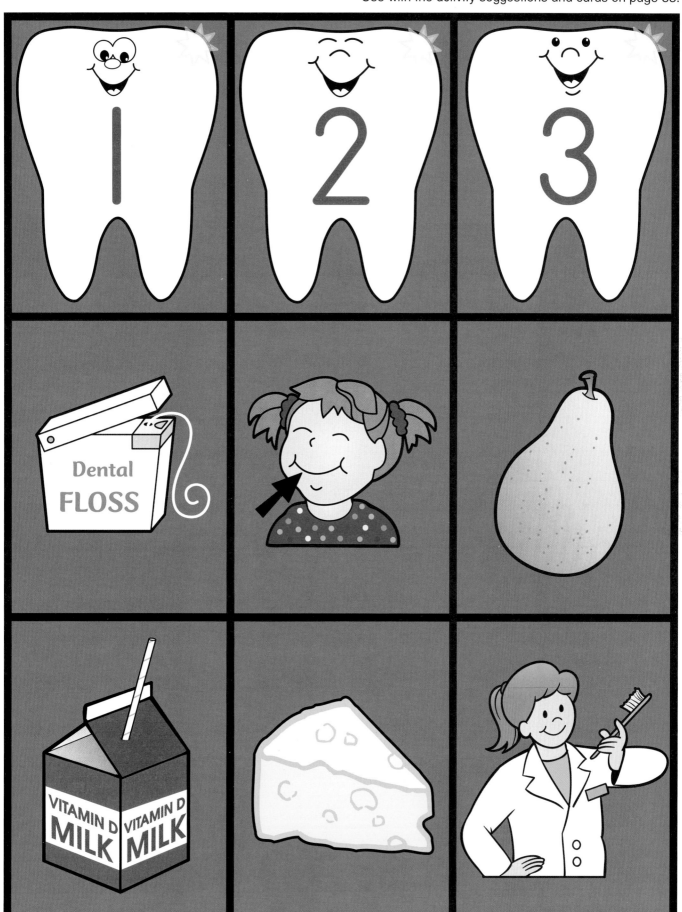

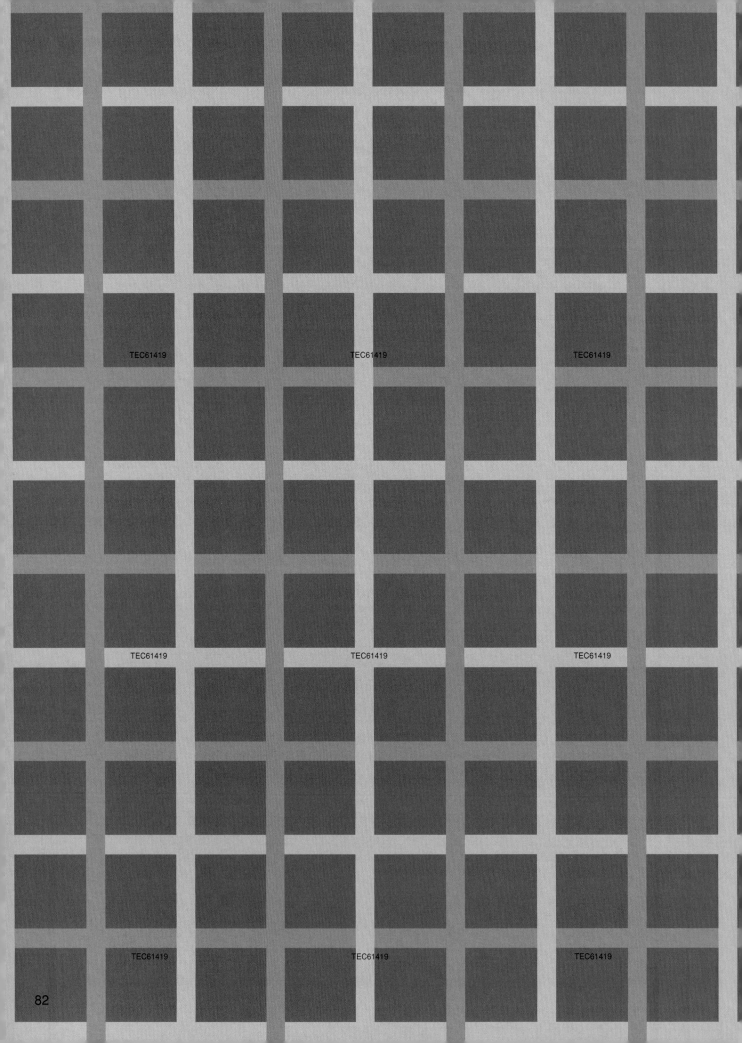

- For a **whole-group** pocket chart activity, put the heading cards in separate rows. Show a picture card. Students identify the item and then pretend to brush across their teeth once for each syllable.

- For a **circle-time** game, put the picture cards in a bag. Students pass the bag and chant, "Brush your teeth every day to help prevent tooth decay!" At the end, the child with the bag takes a card, uses the picture word in a dental health–related sentence (with help as needed), and then puts the card back. Continue with other cards.

- For a **center** activity, set out the heading cards. Stack the picture cards facedown. A child flips a card, claps the syllables in the picture word, and places the card near the appropriate heading card.

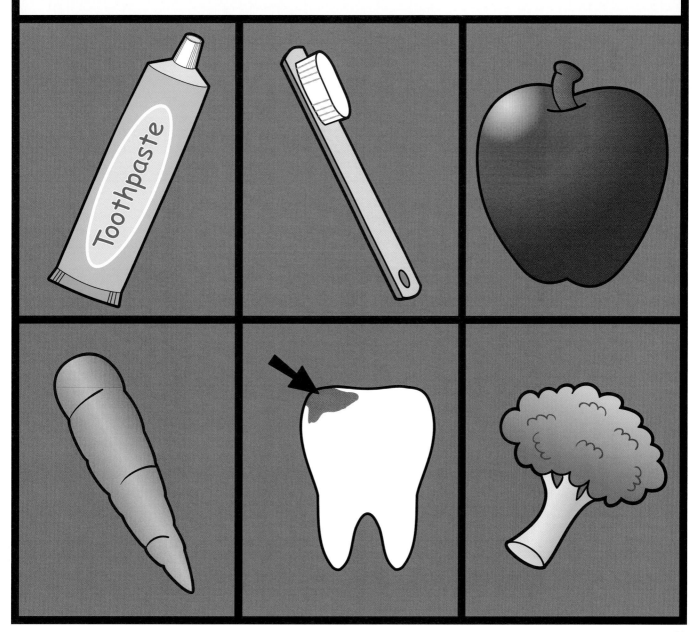

Use with the cards on page 87 for matching games in your pocket chart, Concentration-style games, independent practice, and individual assessment.

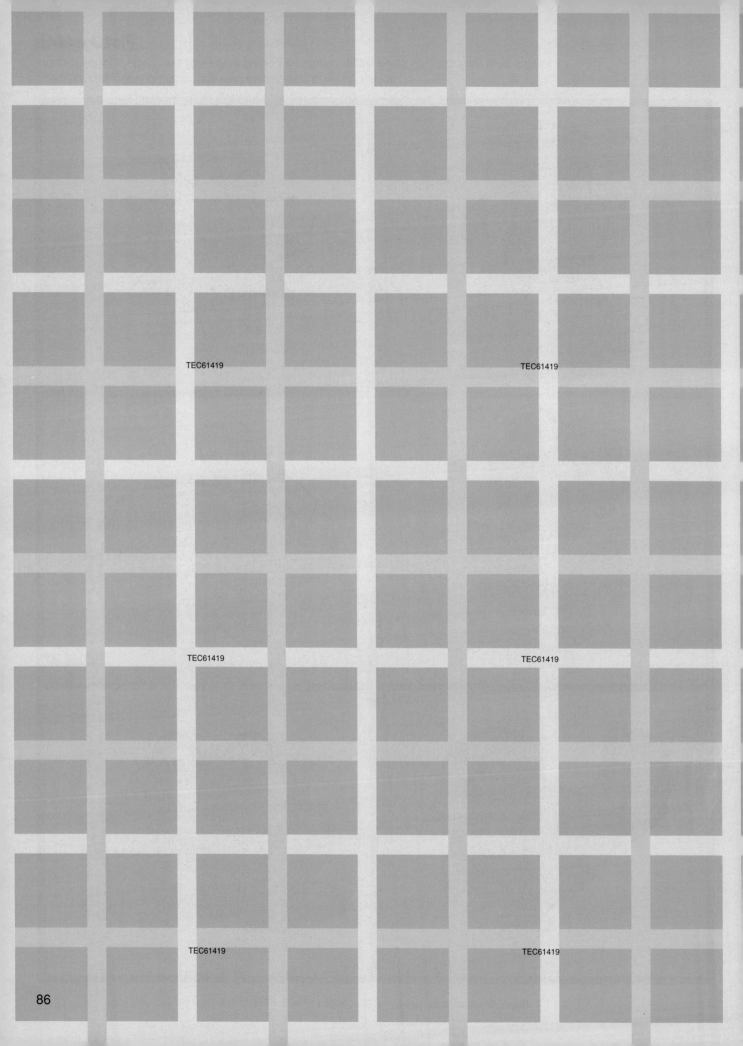

Use with the cards and activity suggestions on page 85.

TEC61419

TEC61419

TEC61419

TEC61419

TEC61419

TEC61419

Valentine Puzzle and Puzzle Base

Use with pages 91 and 93. Remove this page and cut the puzzle (top) from the base (bottom); then cut apart the puzzle pieces along the dashed lines.

TEC61419

TEC61419

TEC61419

TEC61419

TEC61419

TEC61419

TEC61419

Valentine Puzzle and Puzzle Base

Use with pages 89 and 93. Remove this page and cut the puzzle (top) from the base (bottom); then cut apart the puzzle pieces along the dashed lines.

Game Directions and Cards

Use with pages 89 and 91, prepared as described on those pages. Cut apart the cards shown below and put them in a gift bag.

Directions for two players:
1. Choose a puzzle and matching base. Scatter the puzzle pieces faceup.
2. When it is your turn, take a card from the bag and name the shape.
3. If the shape is a heart, match one puzzle piece to your puzzle base. Return the card to the bag.
4. If the shape is not a heart, your turn is over. Return the card to the bag.
5. The first player to put a puzzle together wins!

Who Ate the Candy?

Tell a Story.

Happy Valentine's Day!

1 Beginning

Who ate 's candy?

2 Middle

How does  find out?

3 End

What does   do?

Ready for January & February ·©The Mailbox® Books · TEC61419

Literacy center: Remove this page and put it in a plastic page protector for durability. Set out the page and writing paper. Then have a child dictate or use invented writing to respond question.

Who Ate the Candy?

TEC61419